Hellas. A Lyrical Drama by Percy Bysshe Shelley

A LYRICAL DRAMA.

MANTIS EIM EZTHLON AGONUN. OEDIP. COLON.

"Hellas" was composed at Pisa in the autumn of 1821, and dispatched to London, November 11. It was published, with the author's name, by C. & J. Ollier in the spring of 1822.

Percy Bysshe Shelley is one of the most revered figures in the English poetical landscape. Born on the 4th August 1792 he has, over the years, become rightly regarded as a major Romantic poet. Yet during his own lifetime little of his work was published. Publishers feared his radical views and possible charges against themselves for blasphemy and sedition. On 8th July 1822 a month before his 30th birthday, during a sudden storm, his tragic early death by drowning robbed our culture of many fine expected masterpieces. But in his short spell on earth he weaved much magic. Among his many great works is Hellas, A lyrical drama. Shelley's words are alive with intent, meaning and emotion. A true poet for all our ages.

TO HIS EXCELLENCY, PRINCE ALEXANDER MAVROCORDATO, LATE SECRETARY FOR FOREIGN AFFAIRS TO THE HOSPODAR OF WALLACHIA, THE DRAMA OF HELLAS IS INSCRIBED AS AN IMPERFECT TOKEN OF THE ADMIRATION, SYMPATHY, AND FRIENDSHIP OF THE AUTHOR.
Pisa, November 1, 1821.

Index Of Contents
PREFACE.
PROLOGUE TO HELLAS
DRAMATIS PERSONAE
HELLAS
NOTES

PREFACE.

The poem of "Hellas", written at the suggestion of the events of the moment, is a mere improvise, and derives its interest (should it be found to possess any) solely from the intense sympathy which the Author feels with the cause he would celebrate.

The subject, in its present state, is insusceptible of being treated otherwise than lyrically, and if I have called this poem a drama from the circumstance of its being composed in dialogue, the licence is not greater than that which has been assumed by other poets who have called their productions epics, only because they have been divided into twelve or twenty-four books.

The "Persae" of Aeschylus afforded me the first model of my conception, although the decision of the glorious contest now waging in Greece being yet suspended forbids a catastrophe parallel to the return of Xerxes and the desolation of the Persians. I have, therefore, contented myself with exhibiting a series of lyric pictures, and with having wrought upon the curtain of futurity, which falls upon the unfinished scene, such figures of indistinct and visionary delineation as suggest the final triumph of the Greek cause as a portion of the cause of civilisation and social improvement.

The drama (if drama it must be called) is, however, so inartificial that I doubt whether, if recited on the Thespian waggon to an Athenian village at the Dionysiaca, it would have obtained the prize of the goat. I shall bear with equanimity any punishment, greater than the loss of such a reward, which the Aristarchi of the hour may think fit to inflict.

The only "goat-song" which I have yet attempted has, I confess, in spite of the unfavourable nature of the subject, received a greater and a more valuable portion of applause than I expected or than it deserved.

Common fame is the only authority which I can allege for the details which form the basis of the poem, and I must trespass upon the forgiveness of my readers for the display of newspaper erudition to which I have been reduced. Undoubtedly, until the conclusion of the war, it will be impossible to obtain an account of it sufficiently authentic for historical materials; but poets have their privilege, and it is unquestionable that actions of the most exalted courage have been performed by the Greeks, that they have gained more than one naval victory, and that their defeat in Wallachia was signalized by circumstances of heroism more glorious even than victory.

The apathy of the rulers of the civilised world to the astonishing circumstance of the descendants of that nation to which they owe their civilisation, rising as it were from the ashes of their ruin, is something perfectly inexplicable to a mere spectator of the shows of this mortal scene. We are all Greeks. Our laws, our literature, our religion, our arts have their root in Greece. But for Greece, Rome, the instructor, the conqueror, or the metropolis of our ancestors, would have spread no illumination with her arms, and we might still have been savages and idolaters; or, what is worse, might have arrived at such a stagnant and miserable state of social institution as China and Japan possess.

The human form and the human mind attained to a perfection in Greece which has impressed its image on those faultless productions, whose very fragments are the despair of modern art, and has propagated impulses which cannot cease, through a thousand channels of manifest or imperceptible operation, to ennoble and delight mankind until the extinction of the race.

The modern Greek is the descendant of those glorious beings whom the imagination almost refuses to figure to itself as belonging to our kind, and he inherits much of their sensibility, their rapidity of conception, their enthusiasm, and their courage. If in many instances he is degraded by moral and political slavery to the practice of the basest vices it engenders, and that below the level of ordinary degradation, let us reflect that the corruption of the best produces the worst, and that habits which subsist only in relation to a peculiar state of social institution may be expected to cease as soon as that relation is dissolved. In fact, the Greeks, since the admirable novel of Anastasius could have been a faithful picture of their manners, have undergone most important changes; the flower of their youth, returning to their country from the universities of Italy, Germany, and France, have communicated to their fellow-citizens the latest results of that social perfection of which their ancestors were the original source. The University of Chios contained before the breaking out of the revolution eight hundred students, and among them several Germans and Americans. The munificence and energy of many of the Greek princes and merchants, directed to the renovation of their country with a spirit and a wisdom which has few examples, is above all praise.

The English permit their own oppressors to act according to their natural sympathy with the Turkish tyrant, and to brand upon their name the indelible blot of an alliance with the enemies of domestic happiness, of Christianity and civilisation.

Russia desires to possess, not to liberate Greece; and is contented to see the Turks, its natural enemies, and the Greeks, its intended slaves, enfeeble each other until one or both fall into its net. The wise and generous policy of England would have consisted in establishing the independence of Greece, and in maintaining it both against Russia and the Turk; but when was the oppressor generous or just?

[Should the English people ever become free, they will reflect upon the part which those who presume to represent their will have played in the great drama of the revival of liberty, with feelings which it would become them to anticipate. This is the age of the war of the oppressed against the oppressors, and every one of those ringleaders of the privileged gangs of murderers and swindlers, called Sovereigns, look to each other for aid against the common enemy, and suspend their mutual jealousies in the presence of a mightier fear. Of this holy alliance all the despots of the earth are virtual members. But a new race has arisen throughout Europe, nursed in the abhorrence of the opinions which are its chains, and she will continue to produce fresh generations to accomplish that destiny which tyrants foresee and dread. (This paragraph, suppressed in 1822 by Charles Ollier, was first restored in 1892 by Mr. Buxton Forman ["Poetical Works of P. B. S.", volume 4 pages 40-41] from a proof copy of Hellas in his possession.]

The Spanish Peninsula is already free. France is tranquil in the enjoyment of a partial exemption from the abuses which its unnatural and feeble government are vainly attempting to revive. The seed of blood and misery has been sown in Italy, and a more vigorous race is arising to go forth to the harvest. The world waits only the news of a revolution of Germany to see the tyrants who have pinnacled themselves on its supineness precipitated into the ruin from which they shall never arise. Well do these destroyers of mankind know their enemy, when they impute the insurrection in Greece to the same spirit before which they tremble throughout the rest of Europe, and that enemy well knows the power and the cunning of its opponents, and watches the moment of their approaching weakness and inevitable division to wrest the bloody sceptres from their grasp.

PROLOGUE TO HELLAS

HERALD OF ETERNITY:
It is the day when all the sons of God
Wait in the roofless senate-house, whose floor
Is Chaos, and the immovable abyss
Frozen by His steadfast word to hyaline

The shadow of God, and delegate
Of that before whose breath the universe
Is as a print of dew.
Hierarchs and kings
Who from your thrones pinnacled on the past
Sway the reluctant present, ye who sit
Pavilioned on the radiance or the gloom

Of mortal thought, which like an exhalation
Steaming from earth, conceals the ... of heaven
Which gave it birth. ... assemble here
Before your Father's throne; the swift decree
Yet hovers, and the fiery incarnation
Is yet withheld, clothed in which it shall annul
The fairest of those wandering isles that gem
The sapphire space of interstellar air,
That green and azure sphere, that earth enwrapped
Less in the beauty of its tender light
Than in an atmosphere of living spirit
Which interpenetrating all the ...
it rolls from realm to realm
And age to age, and in its ebb and flow
Impels the generations
To their appointed place,
Whilst the high Arbiter
Beholds the strife, and at the appointed time
Sends His decrees veiled in eternal...

Within the circuit of this pendent orb
There lies an antique region, on which fell
The dews of thought in the world's golden dawn
Earliest and most benign, and from it sprung
Temples and cities and immortal forms
And harmonies of wisdom and of song,
And thoughts, and deeds worthy of thoughts so fair.
And when the sun of its dominion failed,
And when the winter of its glory came,
The winds that stripped it bare blew on and swept
That dew into the utmost wildernesses
In wandering clouds of sunny rain that thawed
The unmaternal bosom of the North.
Haste, sons of God, ... for ye beheld,
Reluctant, or consenting, or astonished,
The stern decrees go forth, which heaped on Greece
Ruin and degradation and despair.
A fourth now waits: assemble, sons of God,
To speed or to prevent or to suspend,
If, as ye dream, such power be not withheld,
The unaccomplished destiny.

CHORUS:
The curtain of the Universe
Is rent and shattered,
The splendour-winged worlds disperse
Like wild doves scattered.

Space is roofless and bare,
And in the midst a cloudy shrine,
Dark amid thrones of light.

In the blue glow of hyaline
Golden worlds revolve and shine.
In ... flight
From every point of the Infinite,
Like a thousand dawns on a single night
The splendours rise and spread;
And through thunder and darkness dread
Light and music are radiated,
And in their pavilioned chariots led
By living wings high overhead
The giant Powers move,
Gloomy or bright as the thrones they fill.

A chaos of light and motion
Upon that glassy ocean.

The senate of the Gods is met,
Each in his rank and station set;
There is silence in the spaces
Lo! Satan, Christ, and Mahomet
Start from their places!

CHRIST:
Almighty Father!
Low-kneeling at the feet of Destiny

There are two fountains in which spirits weep
When mortals err, Discord and Slavery named,
And with their bitter dew two Destinies
Filled each their irrevocable urns; the third
Fiercest and mightiest, mingled both, and added
Chaos and Death, and slow Oblivion's lymph,
And hate and terror, and the poisoned rain

The Aurora of the nations. By this brow
Whose pores wept tears of blood, by these wide wounds,
By this imperial crown of agony,
By infamy and solitude and death,
For this I underwent, and by the pain
Of pity for those who would ... for me
The unremembered joy of a revenge,
For this I felt by Plato's sacred light,
Of which my spirit was a burning morrow
By Greece and all she cannot cease to be.
Her quenchless words, sparks of immortal truth,
Stars of all night, her harmonies and forms,
Echoes and shadows of what Love adores
In thee, I do compel thee, send forth Fate,
Thy irrevocable child: let her descend,
A seraph-winged Victory [arrayed]
In tempest of the omnipotence of God

Which sweeps through all things.

From hollow leagues, from Tyranny which arms
Adverse miscreeds and emulous anarchies
To stamp, as on a winged serpent's seed,
Upon the name of Freedom; from the storm
Of faction, which like earthquake shakes and sickens
The solid heart of enterprise; from all
By which the holiest dreams of highest spirits
Are stars beneath the dawn...
She shall arise
Victorious as the world arose from Chaos!
And as the Heavens and the Earth arrayed
Their presence in the beauty and the light
Of Thy first smile, O Father, as they gather
The spirit of Thy love which paves for them
Their path o'er the abyss, till every sphere
Shall be one living Spirit, so shall Greece

SATAN:
Be as all things beneath the empyrean,
Mine! Art thou eyeless like old Destiny,
Thou mockery-king, crowned with a wreath of thorns?
Whose sceptre is a reed, the broken reed
Which pierces thee! whose throne a chair of scorn;
For seest thou not beneath this crystal floor
The innumerable worlds of golden light
Which are my empire, and the least of them
which thou wouldst redeem from me?
Know'st thou not them my portion?
Or wouldst rekindle the ... strife
Which our great Father then did arbitrate
Which he assigned to his competing sons
Each his apportioned realm?
Thou Destiny,
Thou who art mailed in the omnipotence
Of Him who tends thee forth, whate'er thy task,
Speed, spare not to accomplish, and be mine
Thy trophies, whether Greece again become
The fountain in the desert whence the earth
Shall drink of freedom, which shall give it strength
To suffer, or a gulf of hollow death
To swallow all delight, all life, all hope.
Go, thou Vicegerent of my will, no less
Than of the Father's; but lest thou shouldst faint,
The winged hounds, Famine and Pestilence,
Shall wait on thee, the hundred-forked snake
Insatiate Superstition still shall...
The earth behind thy steps, and War shall hover
Above, and Fraud shall gape below, and Change
Shall flit before thee on her dragon wings,

Convulsing and consuming, and I add
Three vials of the tears which daemons weep
When virtuous spirits through the gate of Death
Pass triumphing over the thorns of life,
Sceptres and crowns, mitres and swords and snares,
Trampling in scorn, like Him and Socrates.
The first is Anarchy; when Power and Pleasure,
Glory and science and security,
On Freedom hang like fruit on the green tree,
Then pour it forth, and men shall gather ashes.
The second Tyranny

CHRIST:
Obdurate spirit!
Thou seest but the Past in the To-come.
Pride is thy error and thy punishment.
Boast not thine empire, dream not that thy worlds
Are more than furnace-sparks or rainbow-drops
Before the Power that wields and kindles them.
True greatness asks not space, true excellence
Lives in the Spirit of all things that live,
Which lends it to the worlds thou callest thine.

MAHOMET:
...Haste thou and fill the waning crescent
With beams as keen as those which pierced the shadow
Of Christian night rolled back upon the West,
When the orient moon of Islam rode in triumph
From Tmolus to the Acroceraunian snow.

Wake, thou Word
Of God, and from the throne of Destiny
Even to the utmost limit of thy way
May Triumph

Be thou a curse on them whose creed
Divides and multiplies the most high God.

DRAMATIS PERSONAE:
MAHMUD.
HASSAN.
DAOOD.
AHASUERUS, A JEW.
CHORUS OF GREEK CAPTIVE WOMEN.
[THE PHANTOM OF MAHOMET II. (OMITTED, EDITION 1822.)]
MESSENGERS, SLAVES, AND ATTENDANTS.

SCENE: CONSTANTINOPLE.

TIME: SUNSET.

HELLAS

SCENE: A TERRACE ON THE SERAGLIO.
MAHMUD SLEEPING,
AN INDIAN SLAVE SITTING BESIDE HIS COUCH.

CHORUS OF GREEK CAPTIVE WOMEN:
We strew these opiate flowers
On thy restless pillow,
They were stripped from Orient bowers,
By the Indian billow.
Be thy sleep
Calm and deep,
Like theirs who fell, not ours who weep!

INDIAN:
Away, unlovely dreams!
Away, false shapes of sleep
Be his, as Heaven seems,
Clear, and bright, and deep!
Soft as love, and calm as death,
Sweet as a summer night without a breath.

CHORUS:
Sleep, sleep! our song is laden
With the soul of slumber;
It was sung by a Samian maiden,
Whose lover was of the number
Who now keep
That calm sleep
Whence none may wake, where none shall weep.

INDIAN:
I touch thy temples pale!
I breathe my soul on thee!
And could my prayers avail,
All my joy should be
Dead, and I would live to weep,
So thou mightst win one hour of quiet sleep.

CHORUS:
Breathe low, low
The spell of the mighty mistress now!
When Conscience lulls her sated snake,
And Tyrants sleep, let Freedom wake.
Breathe low, low
The words which, like secret fire, shall flow
Through the veins of the frozen earth, low, low!

SEMICHORUS 1:
Life may change, but it may fly not;
Hope may vanish, but can die not;
Truth be veiled, but still it burneth;
Love repulsed, but it returneth!

SEMICHORUS 2:
Yet were life a charnel where
Hope lay coffined with Despair;
Yet were truth a sacred lie,
Love were lust

SEMICHORUS 1:
If Liberty
Lent not life its soul of light,
Hope its iris of delight,
Truth its prophet's robe to wear,
Love its power to give and bear.

CHORUS:
In the great morning of the world,
The Spirit of God with might unfurled
The flag of Freedom over Chaos,
And all its banded anarchs fled,
Like vultures frighted from Imaus,
Before an earthquake's tread.
So from Time's tempestuous dawn
Freedom's splendour burst and shone:
Thermopylae and Marathon
Caught like mountains beacon-lighted,
The springing Fire. The winged glory
On Philippi half-alighted,
Like an eagle on a promontory.
Its unwearied wings could fan
The quenchless ashes of Milan.
From age to age, from man to man,
It lived; and lit from land to land
Florence, Albion, Switzerland.

Then night fell; and, as from night,
Reassuming fiery flight,
From the West swift Freedom came,
Against the course of Heaven and doom.
A second sun arrayed in flame,
To burn, to kindle, to illume.
From far Atlantis its young beams
Chased the shadows and the dreams.
France, with all her sanguine steams,
Hid, but quenched it not; again
Through clouds its shafts of glory rain
From utmost Germany to Spain.

As an eagle fed with morning
Scorns the embattled tempest's warning,
When she seeks her aerie hanging
In the mountain-cedar's hair,
And her brood expect the clanging
Of her wings through the wild air,
Sick with famine: Freedom, so
To what of Greece remaineth now
Returns; her hoary ruins glow
Like Orient mountains lost in day;
Beneath the safety of her wings
Her renovated nurslings prey,
And in the naked lightenings
Of truth they purge their dazzled eyes.
Let Freedom leave, where'er she flies,
A Desert, or a Paradise:
Let the beautiful and the brave
Share her glory, or a grave.

SEMICHORUS 1:
With the gifts of gladness
Greece did thy cradle strew;

SEMICHORUS 2:
With the tears of sadness
Greece did thy shroud bedew!

SEMICHORUS 1:
With an orphan's affection
She followed thy bier through Time;

SEMICHORUS 2:
And at thy resurrection
Reappeareth, like thou, sublime!

SEMICHORUS 1:
If Heaven should resume thee,
To Heaven shall her spirit ascend;

SEMICHORUS 2:
If Hell should entomb thee,
To Hell shall her high hearts bend.

SEMICHORUS 1:
If Annihilation

SEMICHORUS 2:
Dust let her glories be!
And a name and a nation
Be forgotten, Freedom, with thee!

INDIAN:
His brow grows darker, breathe not, move not!
He starts, he shudders, ye that love not,
With your panting loud and fast,
Have awakened him at last.

MAHMUD [STARTING FROM HIS SLEEP]:
Man the Seraglio-guard! make fast the gate!
What! from a cannonade of three short hours?
'Tis false! that breach towards the Bosphorus
Cannot be practicable yet, who stirs?
Stand to the match; that when the foe prevails
One spark may mix in reconciling ruin
The conqueror and the conquered! Heave the tower
Into the gap, wrench off the roof!
[ENTER HASSAN.]
Ha! what!
The truth of day lightens upon my dream
And I am Mahmud still.

HASSAN:
Your Sublime Highness
Is strangely moved.

MAHMUD:
The times do cast strange shadows
On those who watch and who must rule their course,
Lest they, being first in peril as in glory,
Be whelmed in the fierce ebb: and these are of them.
Thrice has a gloomy vision hunted me
As thus from sleep into the troubled day;
It shakes me as the tempest shakes the sea,
Leaving no figure upon memory's glass.
Would that no matter. Thou didst say thou knewest
A Jew, whose spirit is a chronicle
Of strange and secret and forgotten things.
I bade thee summon him: 'tis said his tribe
Dream, and are wise interpreters of dreams.

HASSAN:
The Jew of whom I spake is old, so old
He seems to have outlived a world's decay;
The hoary mountains and the wrinkled ocean
Seem younger still than he; his hair and beard
Are whiter than the tempest-sifted snow;
His cold pale limbs and pulseless arteries
Are like the fibres of a cloud instinct
With light, and to the soul that quickens them
Are as the atoms of the mountain-drift
To the winter wind: but from his eye looks forth
A life of unconsumed thought which pierces

The Present, and the Past, and the To-come.
Some say that this is he whom the great prophet
Jesus, the son of Joseph, for his mockery,
Mocked with the curse of immortality.
Some feign that he is Enoch: others dream
He was pre-adamite and has survived
Cycles of generation and of ruin.
The sage, in truth, by dreadful abstinence
And conquering penance of the mutinous flesh,
Deep contemplation, and unwearied study,
In years outstretched beyond the date of man,
May have attained to sovereignty and science
Over those strong and secret things and thoughts
Which others fear and know not.

MAHMUD:
I would talk
With this old Jew.

HASSAN:
Thy will is even now
Made known to him, where he dwells in a sea-cavern
'Mid the Demonesi, less accessible
Than thou or God! He who would question him
Must sail alone at sunset, where the stream
Of Ocean sleeps around those foamless isles,
When the young moon is westering as now,
And evening airs wander upon the wave;
And when the pines of that bee-pasturing isle,
Green Erebinthus, quench the fiery shadow
Of his gilt prow within the sapphire water,
Then must the lonely helmsman cry aloud
'Ahasuerus!' and the caverns round
Will answer 'Ahasuerus!' If his prayer
Be granted, a faint meteor will arise
Lighting him over Marmora, and a wind
Will rush out of the sighing pine-forest,
And with the wind a storm of harmony
Unutterably sweet, and pilot him
Through the soft twilight to the Bosphorus:
Thence at the hour and place and circumstance
Fit for the matter of their conference
The Jew appears. Few dare, and few who dare
Win the desired communion but that shout
Bodes

[A SHOUT WITHIN.]

MAHMUD:
Evil, doubtless; Like all human sounds.
Let me converse with spirits.

HASSAN:
That shout again.

MAHMUD:
This Jew whom thou hast summoned

HASSAN:
Will be here

MAHMUD:
When the omnipotent hour to which are yoked
He, I, and all things shall compel, enough!
Silence those mutineers, that drunken crew,
That crowd about the pilot in the storm.
Ay! strike the foremost shorter by a head!
They weary me, and I have need of rest.
Kinks are like stars, they rise and set, they have
The worship of the world, but no repose.

[EXEUNT SEVERALLY.]

CHORUS:
Worlds on worlds are rolling ever
From creation to decay,
Like the bubbles on a river
Sparkling, bursting, borne away.
But they are still immortal
Who, through birth's orient portal
And death's dark chasm hurrying to and fro,
Clothe their unceasing flight
In the brief dust and light
Gathered around their chariots as they go;
New shapes they still may weave,
New gods, new laws receive,
Bright or dim are they as the robes they last
On Death's bare ribs had cast.

A power from the unknown God,
A Promethean conqueror, came;
Like a triumphal path he trod
The thorns of death and shame.
A mortal shape to him
Was like the vapour dim
Which the orient planet animates with light;
Hell, Sin, and Slavery came,
Like bloodhounds mild and tame,
Nor preyed, until their Lord had taken flight;
The moon of Mahomet
Arose, and it shall set:
While blazoned as on Heaven's immortal noon

The cross leads generations on.

Swift as the radiant shapes of sleep
From one whose dreams are Paradise
Fly, when the fond wretch wakes to weep,
And Day peers forth with her blank eyes;
So fleet, so faint, so fair,
The Powers of earth and air
Fled from the folding-star of Bethlehem:
Apollo, Pan, and Love,
And even Olympian Jove
Grew weak, for killing Truth had glared on them;
Our hills and seas and streams,
Dispeopled of their dreams,
Their waters turned to blood, their dew to tears,
Wailed for the golden years.

[ENTER MAHMUD, HASSAN, DAOOD, AND OTHERS.]

MAHMUD:
More gold? our ancestors bought gold with victory,
And shall I sell it for defeat?

DAOOD:
The Janizars
Clamour for pay.

MAHMUD:
Go! bid them pay themselves
With Christian blood! Are there no Grecian virgins
Whose shrieks and spasms and tears they may enjoy?
No infidel children to impale on spears?
No hoary priests after that Patriarch
Who bent the curse against his country's heart,
Which clove his own at last? Go! bid them kill,
Blood is the seed of gold.

DAOOD:
It has been sown,
And yet the harvest to the sicklemen
Is as a grain to each.

MAHMUD:
Then, take this signet,
Unlock the seventh chamber in which lie
The treasures of victorious Solyman,
An empire's spoil stored for a day of ruin.
O spirit of my sires! is it not come?
The prey-birds and the wolves are gorged and sleep;
But these, who spread their feast on the red earth,
Hunger for gold, which fills not. See them fed;

Then, lead them to the rivers of fresh death.
[EXIT DAOOD.]
O miserable dawn, after a night
More glorious than the day which it usurped!
O faith in God! O power on earth! O word
Of the great prophet, whose o'ershadowing wings
Darkened the thrones and idols of the West,
Now bright! For thy sake cursed be the hour,
Even as a father by an evil child,
When the orient moon of Islam rolled in triumph
From Caucasus to White Ceraunia!
Ruin above, and anarchy below;
Terror without, and treachery within;
The Chalice of destruction full, and all
Thirsting to drink; and who among us dares
To dash it from his lips? and where is Hope?

HASSAN:
The lamp of our dominion still rides high;
One God is God, Mahomet is His prophet.
Four hundred thousand Moslems, from the limits
Of utmost Asia, irresistibly
Throng, like full clouds at the Sirocco's cry;
But not like them to weep their strength in tears:
They bear destroying lightning, and their step
Wakes earthquake to consume and overwhelm,
And reign in ruin. Phrygian Olympus,
Tmolus, and Latmos, and Mycale, roughen
With horrent arms; and lofty ships even now,
Like vapours anchored to a mountain's edge,
Freighted with fire and whirlwind, wait at Scala
The convoy of the ever-veering wind.
Samos is drunk with blood; the Greek has paid
Brief victory with swift loss and long despair.
The false Moldavian serfs fled fast and far
When the fierce shout of 'Allah-illa-Allah!'
Rose like the war-cry of the northern wind
Which kills the sluggish clouds, and leaves a flock
Of wild swans struggling with the naked storm.
So were the lost Greeks on the Danube's day!
If night is mute, yet the returning sun
Kindles the voices of the morning birds;
Nor at thy bidding less exultingly
Than birds rejoicing in the golden day,
The Anarchies of Africa unleash
Their tempest-winged cities of the sea,
To speak in thunder to the rebel world.
Like sulphurous clouds, half-shattered by the storm,
They sweep the pale Aegean, while the Queen
Of Ocean, bound upon her island-throne,
Far in the West, sits mourning that her sons

Who frown on Freedom spare a smile for thee:
Russia still hovers, as an eagle might
Within a cloud, near which a kite and crane
Hang tangled in inextricable fight,
To stoop upon the victor; for she fears
The name of Freedom, even as she hates thine.
But recreant Austria loves thee as the Grave
Loves Pestilence, and her slow dogs of war
Fleshed with the chase, come up from Italy,
And howl upon their limits; for they see
The panther, Freedom, fled to her old cover,
Amid seas and mountains, and a mightier brood
Crouch round. What Anarch wears a crown or mitre,
Or bears the sword, or grasps the key of gold,
Whose friends are not thy friends, whose foes thy foes?
Our arsenals and our armouries are full;
Our forts defy assault; ten thousand cannon
Lie ranged upon the beach, and hour by hour
Their earth-convulsing wheels affright the city;
The galloping of fiery steeds makes pale
The Christian merchant; and the yellow Jew
Hides his hoard deeper in the faithless earth.
Like clouds, and like the shadows of the clouds,
Over the hills of Anatolia,
Swift in wide troops the Tartar chivalry
Sweep; the far flashing of their starry lances
Reverberates the dying light of day.
We have one God, one King, one Hope, one Law;
But many-headed Insurrection stands
Divided in itself, and soon must fall.

MAHMUD:
Proud words, when deeds come short, are seasonable:
Look, Hassan, on yon crescent moon, emblazoned
Upon that shattered flag of fiery cloud
Which leads the rear of the departing day;
Wan emblem of an empire fading now!
See how it trembles in the blood-red air,
And like a mighty lamp whose oil is spent
Shrinks on the horizon's edge, while, from above,
One star with insolent and victorious light
Hovers above its fall, and with keen beams,
Like arrows through a fainting antelope,
Strikes its weak form to death.

HASSAN:
Even as that moon
Renews itself

MAHMUD:
Shall we be not renewed!

Far other bark than ours were needed now
To stem the torrent of descending time:
The Spirit that lifts the slave before his lord
Stalks through the capitals of armed kings,
And spreads his ensign in the wilderness:
Exults in chains; and, when the rebel falls,
Cries like the blood of Abel from the dust;
And the inheritors of the earth, like beasts
When earthquake is unleashed, with idiot fear
Cower in their kingly dens as I do now.
What were Defeat when Victory must appal?
Or Danger, when Security looks pale?
How said the messenger, who, from the fort
Islanded in the Danube, saw the battle
Of Bucharest? That -

HASSAN:
Ibrahim's scimitar
Drew with its gleam swift victory from Heaven,
To burn before him in the night of battle
A light and a destruction.

MAHMUD:
Ay! the day
Was ours: but how?

HASSAN:
The light Wallachians,
The Arnaut, Servian, and Albanian allies
Fled from the glance of our artillery
Almost before the thunderstone alit.
One half the Grecian army made a bridge
Of safe and slow retreat, with Moslem dead;
The other

MAHMUD:
Speak, tremble not.

HASSAN:
Islanded
By victor myriads, formed in hollow square
With rough and steadfast front, and thrice flung back
The deluge of our foaming cavalry;
Thrice their keen wedge of battle pierced our lines.
Our baffled army trembled like one man
Before a host, and gave them space; but soon,
From the surrounding hills, the batteries blazed,
Kneading them down with fire and iron rain:
Yet none approached; till, like a field of corn
Under the hook of the swart sickleman,
The band, intrenched in mounds of Turkish dead,

Grew weak and few. Then said the Pacha, 'Slaves,
Render yourselves, they have abandoned you
What hope of refuge, or retreat, or aid?
We grant your lives.' 'Grant that which is thine own!'
Cried one, and fell upon his sword and died!
Another 'God, and man, and hope abandon me;
But I to them, and to myself, remain
Constant:' he bowed his head, and his heart burst.
A third exclaimed, 'There is a refuge, tyrant,
Where thou darest not pursue, and canst not harm
Shouldst thou pursue; there we shall meet again.'
Then held his breath, and, after a brief spasm,
The indignant spirit cast its mortal garment
Among the slain, dead earth upon the earth!
So these survivors, each by different ways,
Some strange, all sudden, none dishonourable,
Met in triumphant death; and when our army
Closed in, while yet wonder, and awe, and shame
Held back the base hyaenas of the battle
That feed upon the dead and fly the living,
One rose out of the chaos of the slain:
And if it were a corpse which some dread spirit
Of the old saviours of the land we rule
Had lifted in its anger, wandering by;
Or if there burned within the dying man
Unquenchable disdain of death, and faith
Creating what it feigned; I cannot tell
But he cried, 'Phantoms of the free, we come!
Armies of the Eternal, ye who strike
To dust the citadels of sanguine kings,
And shake the souls throned on their stony hearts,
And thaw their frostwork diadems like dew;
O ye who float around this clime, and weave
The garment of the glory which it wears,
Whose fame, though earth betray the dust it clasped,
Lies sepulchred in monumental thought;
Progenitors of all that yet is great,
Ascribe to your bright senate, O accept
In your high ministrations, us, your sons
Us first, and the more glorious yet to come!
And ye, weak conquerors! giants who look pale
When the crushed worm rebels beneath your tread,
The vultures and the dogs, your pensioners tame,
Are overgorged; but, like oppressors, still
They crave the relic of Destruction's feast.
The exhalations and the thirsty winds
Are sick with blood; the dew is foul with death;
Heaven's light is quenched in slaughter: thus, where'er
Upon your camps, cities, or towers, or fleets,
The obscene birds the reeking remnants cast
Of these dead limbs, upon your streams and mountains,

Upon your fields, your gardens, and your housetops,
Where'er the winds shall creep, or the clouds fly,
Or the dews fall, or the angry sun look down
With poisoned light, Famine, and Pestilence,
And Panic, shall wage war upon our side!
Nature from all her boundaries is moved
Against ye: Time has found ye light as foam.
The Earth rebels; and Good and Evil stake
Their empire o'er the unborn world of men
On this one cast; but ere the die be thrown,
The renovated genius of our race,
Proud umpire of the impious game, descends,
A seraph-winged Victory, bestriding
The tempest of the Omnipotence of God,
Which sweeps all things to their appointed doom,
And you to oblivion!' More he would have said,
But -

MAHMUD:
Died, as thou shouldst ore thy lips had painted
Their ruin in the hues of our success.
A rebel's crime, gilt with a rebel's tongue!
Your heart is Greek, Hassan.

HASSAN:
It may be so:
A spirit not my own wrenched me within,
And I have spoken words I fear and hate;
Yet would I die for -

MAHMUD:
Live! oh live! outlive
Me and this sinking empire. But the fleet

HASSAN:
Alas!

MAHMUD:
The fleet which, like a flock of clouds
Chased by the wind, flies the insurgent banner!
Our winged castles from their merchant ships!
Our myriads before their weak pirate bands!
Our arms before their chains! our years of empire
Before their centuries of servile fear!
Death is awake! Repulse is on the waters!
They own no more the thunder-bearing banner
Of Mahmud; but, like hounds of a base breed,
Gorge from a stranger's hand, and rend their master.

HASSAN:
Latmos, and Ampelos, and Phanae saw

The wreck -

MAHMUD:
The caves of the Icarian isles
Told each to the other in loud mockery,
And with the tongue as of a thousand echoes,
First of the sea-convulsing fight and, then,
Thou darest to speak, senseless are the mountains:
Interpret thou their voice!

HASSAN:
My presence bore
A part in that day's shame. The Grecian fleet
Bore down at daybreak from the North, and hung
As multitudinous on the ocean line,
As cranes upon the cloudless Thracian wind.
Our squadron, convoying ten thousand men,
Was stretching towards Nauplia when the battle
Was kindled.
First through the hail of our artillery
The agile Hydriote barks with press of sail
Dashed: ship to ship, cannon to cannon, man
To man were grappled in the embrace of war,
Inextricable but by death or victory.
The tempest of the raging fight convulsed
To its crystalline depths that stainless sea,
And shook Heaven's roof of golden morning clouds,
Poised on an hundred azure mountain-isles.
In the brief trances of the artillery
One cry from the destroyed and the destroyer
Rose, and a cloud of desolation wrapped
The unforeseen event, till the north wind
Sprung from the sea, lifting the heavy veil
Of battle-smoke, then victory, victory!
For, as we thought, three frigates from Algiers
Bore down from Naxos to our aid, but soon
The abhorred cross glimmered behind, before,
Among, around us; and that fatal sign
Dried with its beams the strength in Moslem hearts,
As the sun drinks the dew. What more? We fled!
Our noonday path over the sanguine foam
Was beaconed, and the glare struck the sun pale,
By our consuming transports: the fierce light
Made all the shadows of our sails blood-red,
And every countenance blank. Some ships lay feeding
The ravening fire, even to the water's level;
Some were blown up; some, settling heavily,
Sunk; and the shrieks of our companions died
Upon the wind, that bore us fast and far,
Even after they were dead. Nine thousand perished!
We met the vultures legioned in the air

Stemming the torrent of the tainted wind;
They, screaming from their cloudy mountain-peaks,
Stooped through the sulphurous battle-smoke and perched
Each on the weltering carcase that we loved,
Like its ill angel or its damned soul,
Riding upon the bosom of the sea.
We saw the dog-fish hastening to their feast.
Joy waked the voiceless people of the sea,
And ravening Famine left his ocean cave
To dwell with War, with us, and with Despair.
We met night three hours to the west of Patmos,
And with night, tempest

MAHMUD:
Cease!

[ENTER A MESSENGER.]

MESSENGER:
Your Sublime Highness,
That Christian hound, the Muscovite Ambassador,
Has left the city. If the rebel fleet
Had anchored in the port, had victory
Crowned the Greek legions in the Hippodrome,
Panic were tamer. Obedience and Mutiny,
Like giants in contention planet-struck,
Stand gazing on each other. There is peace
In Stamboul.

MAHMUD:
Is the grave not calmer still?
Its ruins shall be mine.

HASSAN:
Fear not the Russian:
The tiger leagues not with the stag at bay
Against the hunter. Cunning, base, and cruel,
He crouches, watching till the spoil be won,
And must be paid for his reserve in blood.
After the war is fought, yield the sleek Russian
That which thou canst not keep, his deserved portion
Of blood, which shall not flow through streets and fields,
Rivers and seas, like that which we may win,
But stagnate in the veins of Christian slaves!

[ENTER SECOND MESSENGER.]

SECOND MESSENGER:
Nauplia, Tripolizza, Mothon, Athens,
Navarin, Artas, Monembasia,
Corinth, and Thebes are carried by assault,

And every Islamite who made his dogs
Fat with the flesh of Galilean slaves
Passed at the edge of the sword: the lust of blood,
Which made our warriors drunk, is quenched in death;
But like a fiery plague breaks out anew
In deeds which make the Christian cause look pale
In its own light. The garrison of Patras
Has store but for ten days, nor is there hope
But from the Briton: at once slave and tyrant,
His wishes still are weaker than his fears,
Or he would sell what faith may yet remain
From the oaths broke in Genoa and in Norway;
And if you buy him not, your treasury
Is empty even of promises, his own coin.
The freedman of a western poet-chief
Holds Attica with seven thousand rebels,
And has beat back the Pacha of Negropont:
The aged Ali sits in Yanina
A crownless metaphor of empire:
His name, that shadow of his withered might,
Holds our besieging army like a spell
In prey to famine, pest, and mutiny;
He, bastioned in his citadel, looks forth
Joyless upon the sapphire lake that mirrors
The ruins of the city where he reigned
Childless and sceptreless. The Greek has reaped
The costly harvest his own blood matured,
Not the sower, Ali, who has bought a truce
From Ypsilanti with ten camel-loads
Of Indian gold.

[ENTER A THIRD MESSENGER.]

MAHMUD:
What more?

THIRD MESSENGER:
The Christian tribes
Of Lebanon and the Syrian wilderness
Are in revolt; Damascus, Hems, Aleppo
Tremble; the Arab menaces Medina,
The Aethiop has intrenched himself in Sennaar,
And keeps the Egyptian rebel well employed,
Who denies homage, claims investiture
As price of tardy aid. Persia demands
The cities on the Tigris, and the Georgians
Refuse their living tribute. Crete and Cyprus,
Like mountain-twins that from each other's veins
Catch the volcano-fire and earthquake-spasm,
Shake in the general fever. Through the city,
Like birds before a storm, the Santons shriek,

And prophesyings horrible and new
Are heard among the crowd: that sea of men
Sleeps on the wrecks it made, breathless and still.
A Dervise, learned in the Koran, preaches
That it is written how the sins of Islam
Must raise up a destroyer even now.
The Greeks expect a Saviour from the West,
Who shall not come, men say, in clouds and glory,
But in the omnipresence of that Spirit
In which all live and are. Ominous signs
Are blazoned broadly on the noonday sky:
One saw a red cross stamped upon the sun;
It has rained blood; and monstrous births declare
The secret wrath of Nature and her Lord.
The army encamped upon the Cydaris
Was roused last night by the alarm of battle,
And saw two hosts conflicting in the air,
The shadows doubtless of the unborn time
Cast on the mirror of the night. While yet
The fight hung balanced, there arose a storm
Which swept the phantoms from among the stars.
At the third watch the Spirit of the Plague
Was heard abroad flapping among the tents;
Those who relieved watch found the sentinels dead.
The last news from the camp is, that a thousand
Have sickened, and

[ENTER A FOURTH MESSENGER.]

MAHMUD:
And thou, pale ghost, dim shadow
Of some untimely rumour, speak!

FOURTH MESSENGER:
One comes
Fainting with toil, covered with foam and blood:
He stood, he says, on Chelonites'
Promontory, which o'erlooks the isles that groan
Under the Briton's frown, and all their waters
Then trembling in the splendour of the moon,
When as the wandering clouds unveiled or hid
Her boundless light, he saw two adverse fleets
Stalk through the night in the horizon's glimmer,
Mingling fierce thunders and sulphureous gleams,
And smoke which strangled every infant wind
That soothed the silver clouds through the deep air.
At length the battle slept, but the Sirocco
Awoke, and drove his flock of thunder-clouds
Over the sea-horizon, blotting out
All objects, save that in the faint moon-glimpse
He saw, or dreamed he saw, the Turkish admiral

And two the loftiest of our ships of war,
With the bright image of that Queen of Heaven,
Who hid, perhaps, her face for grief, reversed;
And the abhorred cross

[ENTER AN ATTENDANT.]

ATTENDANT:
Your Sublime Highness,
The Jew, who

MAHMUD:
Could not come more seasonably:
Bid him attend. I'll hear no more! too long
We gaze on danger through the mist of fear,
And multiply upon our shattered hopes
The images of ruin. Come what will!
To-morrow and to-morrow are as lamps
Set in our path to light us to the edge
Through rough and smooth, nor can we suffer aught
Which He inflicts not in whose hand we are.

[EXEUNT.]

SEMICHORUS 1:
Would I were the winged cloud
Of a tempest swift and loud!
I would scorn
The smile of morn
And the wave where the moonrise is born!
I would leave
The spirits of eve
A shroud for the corpse of the day to weave
From other threads than mine!
Bask in the deep blue noon divine.
Who would? Not I.

SEMICHORUS 2:
Whither to fly?

SEMICHORUS 1:
Where the rocks that gird th' Aegean
Echo to the battle paean
Of the free
I would flee
A tempestuous herald of victory!
My golden rain
For the Grecian slain
Should mingle in tears with the bloody main,
And my solemn thunder-knell
Should ring to the world the passing-bell

Of Tyranny!

SEMICHORUS 2:
Ah king! wilt thou chain
The rack and the rain?
Wilt thou fetter the lightning and hurricane?
The storms are free,
But we

CHORUS:
O Slavery! thou frost of the world's prime,
Killing its flowers and leaving its thorns bare!
Thy touch has stamped these limbs with crime,
These brows thy branding garland bear,
But the free heart, the impassive soul
Scorn thy control!

SEMICHORUS 1:
Let there be light! said Liberty,
And like sunrise from the sea,
Athens arose! Around her born,
Shone like mountains in the morn
Glorious states; and are they now
Ashes, wrecks, oblivion?

SEMICHORUS 2:
Go,
Where Thermae and Asopus swallowed
Persia, as the sand does foam:
Deluge upon deluge followed,
Discord, Macedon, and Rome:
And lastly thou!

SEMICHORUS 1:
Temples and towers,
Citadels and marts, and they
Who live and die there, have been ours,
And may be thine, and must decay;
But Greece and her foundations are
Built below the tide of war,
Based on the crystalline sea
Of thought and its eternity;
Her citizens, imperial spirits,
Rule the present from the past,
On all this world of men inherits
Their seal is set.

SEMICHORUS 2:
Hear ye the blast,
Whose Orphic thunder thrilling calls
From ruin her Titanian walls?

Whose spirit shakes the sapless bones
Of Slavery? Argos, Corinth, Crete
Hear, and from their mountain thrones
The daemons and the nymphs repeat
The harmony.

SEMICHORUS 1:
I hear! I hear!

SEMICHORUS 2:
The world's eyeless charioteer,
Destiny, is hurrying by!
What faith is crushed, what empire bleeds
Beneath her earthquake-footed steeds?
What eagle-winged victory sits
At her right hand? what shadow flits
Before? what splendour rolls behind?
Ruin and renovation cry
'Who but We?'

SEMICHORUS 1:
I hear! I hear!
The hiss as of a rushing wind,
The roar as of an ocean foaming,
The thunder as of earthquake coming.
I hear! I hear!
The crash as of an empire falling,
The shrieks as of a people calling
'Mercy! mercy!' How they thrill!
Then a shout of 'kill! kill! kill!'
And then a small still voice, thus

SEMICHORUS 2:
For
Revenge and Wrong bring forth their kind,
The foul cubs like their parents are,
Their den is in the guilty mind,
And Conscience feeds them with despair.

SEMICHORUS 1:
In sacred Athens, near the fane
Of Wisdom, Pity's altar stood:
Serve not the unknown God in vain.
But pay that broken shrine again,
Love for hate and tears for blood.

[ENTER MAHMUD AND AHASUERUS.]

MAHMUD:
Thou art a man, thou sayest, even as we.

AHASUERUS:
No more!

MAHMUD:
But raised above thy fellow-men
By thought, as I by power.

AHASUERUS:
Thou sayest so.

MAHMUD:
Thou art an adept in the difficult lore
Of Greek and Frank philosophy; thou numberest
The flowers, and thou measurest the stars;
Thou severest element from element;
Thy spirit is present in the Past, and sees
The birth of this old world through all its cycles
Of desolation and of loveliness,
And when man was not, and how man became
The monarch and the slave of this low sphere,
And all its narrow circles, it is much
I honour thee, and would be what thou art
Were I not what I am; but the unborn hour,
Cradled in fear and hope, conflicting storms,
Who shall unveil? Nor thou, nor I, nor any
Mighty or wise. I apprehended not
What thou hast taught me, but I now perceive
That thou art no interpreter of dreams;
Thou dost not own that art, device, or God,
Can make the Future present, let it come!
Moreover thou disdainest us and ours;
Thou art as God, whom thou contemplatest.

AHASUERUS:
Disdain thee? not the worm beneath thy feet!
The Fathomless has care for meaner things
Than thou canst dream, and has made pride for those
Who would be what they may not, or would seem
That which they are not. Sultan! talk no more
Of thee and me, the Future and the Past;
But look on that which cannot change the One,
The unborn and the undying. Earth and ocean,
Space, and the isles of life or light that gem
The sapphire floods of interstellar air,
This firmament pavilioned upon chaos,
With all its cressets of immortal fire,
Whose outwall, bastioned impregnably
Against the escape of boldest thoughts, repels them
As Calpe the Atlantic clouds, this Whole
Of suns, and worlds, and men, and beasts, and flowers,
With all the silent or tempestuous workings

By which they have been, are, or cease to be,
Is but a vision; all that it inherits
Are motes of a sick eye, bubbles and dreams;
Thought is its cradle and its grave, nor less
The Future and the Past are idle shadows
Of thought's eternal flight, they have no being:
Nought is but that which feels itself to be.

MAHMUD:
What meanest thou? Thy words stream like a tempest
Of dazzling mist within my brain, they shake
The earth on which I stand, and hang like night
On Heaven above me. What can they avail?
They cast on all things surest, brightest, best,
Doubt, insecurity, astonishment.

AHASUERUS:
Mistake me not! All is contained in each.
Dodona's forest to an acorn's cup
Is that which has been, or will be, to that
Which is, the absent to the present. Thought
Alone, and its quick elements, Will, Passion,
Reason, Imagination, cannot die;
They are, what that which they regard appears,
The stuff whence mutability can weave
All that it hath dominion o'er, worlds, worms,
Empires, and superstitions. What has thought
To do with time, or place, or circumstance?
Wouldst thou behold the Future? ask and have!
Knock and it shall be opened, look, and lo!
The coming age is shadowed on the Past
As on a glass.

MAHMUD:
Wild, wilder thoughts convulse
My spirit. Did not Mahomet the Second
Win Stamboul?

AHASUERUS:
Thou wouldst ask that giant spirit
The written fortunes of thy house and faith.
Thou wouldst cite one out of the grave to tell
How what was born in blood must die.

MAHMUD:
Thy words
Have power on me! I see

AHASUERUS:
What hearest thou?

MAHMUD:
A far whisper
Terrible silence.

AHASUERUS:
What succeeds?

MAHMUD:
The sound
As of the assault of an imperial city,
The hiss of inextinguishable fire,
The roar of giant cannon; the earthquaking
Fall of vast bastions and precipitous towers,
The shock of crags shot from strange enginery,
The clash of wheels, and clang of armed hoofs,
And crash of brazen mail as of the wreck
Of adamantine mountains, the mad blast
Of trumpets, and the neigh of raging steeds,
The shrieks of women whose thrill jars the blood,
And one sweet laugh, most horrible to hear,
As of a joyous infant waked and playing
With its dead mother's breast, and now more loud
The mingled battle-cry, ha! hear I not
'En touto nike!' 'Allah-illa-Allah!'?

AHASUERUS:
The sulphurous mist is raised, thou seest

MAHMUD:
A chasm,
As of two mountains in the wall of Stamboul;
And in that ghastly breach the Islamites,
Like giants on the ruins of a world,
Stand in the light of sunrise. In the dust
Glimmers a kingless diadem, and one
Of regal port has cast himself beneath
The stream of war. Another proudly clad
In golden arms spurs a Tartarian barb
Into the gap, and with his iron mace
Directs the torrent of that tide of men,
And seems, he is, Mahomet!

AHASUERUS:
What thou seest
Is but the ghost of thy forgotten dream.
A dream itself, yet less, perhaps, than that
Thou call'st reality. Thou mayst behold
How cities, on which Empire sleeps enthroned,
Bow their towered crests to mutability.
Poised by the flood, e'en on the height thou holdest,
Thou mayst now learn how the full tide of power

Ebbs to its depths. Inheritor of glory,
Conceived in darkness, born in blood, and nourished
With tears and toil, thou seest the mortal throes
Of that whose birth was but the same. The Past
Now stands before thee like an Incarnation
Of the To-come; yet wouldst thou commune with
That portion of thyself which was ere thou
Didst start for this brief race whose crown is death,
Dissolve with that strong faith and fervent passion
Which called it from the uncreated deep,
Yon cloud of war, with its tempestuous phantoms
Of raging death; and draw with mighty will
The imperial shade hither.

[EXIT AHASUERUS.]

[THE PHANTOM OF MAHOMET THE SECOND APPEARS.]

MAHMUD:
Approach!

PHANTOM:
I come
Thence whither thou must go! The grave is fitter
To take the living than give up the dead;
Yet has thy faith prevailed, and I am here.
The heavy fragments of the power which fell
When I arose, like shapeless crags and clouds,
Hang round my throne on the abyss, and voices
Of strange lament soothe my supreme repose,
Wailing for glory never to return.
A later Empire nods in its decay:
The autumn of a greener faith is come,
And wolfish change, like winter, howls to strip
The foliage in which Fame, the eagle, built
Her aerie, while Dominion whelped below.
The storm is in its branches, and the frost
Is on its leaves, and the blank deep expects
Oblivion on oblivion, spoil on spoil,
Ruin on ruin: Thou art slow, my son;
The Anarchs of the world of darkness keep
A throne for thee, round which thine empire lies
Boundless and mute; and for thy subjects thou,
Like us, shalt rule the ghosts of murdered life,
The phantoms of the powers who rule thee now
Mutinous passions, and conflicting fears,
And hopes that sate themselves on dust, and die!
Stripped of their mortal strength, as thou of thine.
Islam must fall, but we will reign together
Over its ruins in the world of death:
And if the trunk be dry, yet shall the seed

Unfold itself even in the shape of that
Which gathers birth in its decay. Woe! woe!
To the weak people tangled in the grasp
Of its last spasms.

MAHMUD:
Spirit, woe to all!
Woe to the wronged and the avenger! Woe
To the destroyer, woe to the destroyed!
Woe to the dupe, and woe to the deceiver!
Woe to the oppressed, and woe to the oppressor!
Woe both to those that suffer and inflict;
Those who are born and those who die! but say,
Imperial shadow of the thing I am,
When, how, by whom, Destruction must accomplish
Her consummation!

PHANTOM:
Ask the cold pale Hour,
Rich in reversion of impending death,
When HE shall fall upon whose ripe gray hairs
Sit Care, and Sorrow, and Infirmity
The weight which Crime, whose wings are plumed with years,
Leaves in his flight from ravaged heart to heart
Over the heads of men, under which burthen
They bow themselves unto the grave: fond wretch!
He leans upon his crutch, and talks of years
To come, and how in hours of youth renewed
He will renew lost joys, and

VOICE WITHOUT:
Victory! Victory!

[THE PHANTOM VANISHES.]

MAHMUD:
What sound of the importunate earth has broken
My mighty trance?

VOICE WITHOUT:
Victory! Victory!

MAHMUD:
Weak lightning before darkness! poor faint smile
Of dying Islam! Voice which art the response
Of hollow weakness! Do I wake and live?
Were there such things, or may the unquiet brain,
Vexed by the wise mad talk of the old Jew,
Have shaped itself these shadows of its fear?
It matters not! for nought we see or dream,
Possess, or lose, or grasp at, can be worth

More than it gives or teaches. Come what may,
The Future must become the Past, and I
As they were to whom once this present hour,
This gloomy crag of time to which I cling,
Seemed an Elysian isle of peace and joy
Never to be attained. I must rebuke
This drunkenness of triumph ere it die,
And dying, bring despair. Victory! poor slaves!

[EXIT MAHMUD.]

VOICE WITHOUT:
Shout in the jubilee of death! The Greeks
Are as a brood of lions in the net
Round which the kingly hunters of the earth
Stand smiling. Anarchs, ye whose daily food
Are curses, groans, and gold, the fruit of death,
From Thule to the girdle of the world,
Come, feast! the board groans with the flesh of men;
The cup is foaming with a nation's blood,
Famine and Thirst await! eat, drink, and die!

SEMICHORUS 1:
Victorious Wrong, with vulture scream,
Salutes the rising sun, pursues the flying day!
I saw her, ghastly as a tyrant's dream,
Perch on the trembling pyramid of night,
Beneath which earth and all her realms pavilioned lay
In visions of the dawning undelight.
Who shall impede her flight?
Who rob her of her prey?

VOICE WITHOUT:
Victory! Victory! Russia's famished eagles
Dare not to prey beneath the crescent's light.
Impale the remnant of the Greeks! despoil!
Violate! make their flesh cheaper than dust!

SEMICHORUS 2:
Thou voice which art
The herald of the ill in splendour hid!
Thou echo of the hollow heart
Of monarchy, bear me to thine abode
When desolation flashes o'er a world destroyed:
Oh, bear me to those isles of jagged cloud
Which float like mountains on the earthquake, mid
The momentary oceans of the lightning,
Or to some toppling promontory proud
Of solid tempest whose black pyramid,
Riven, overhangs the founts intensely bright'ning
Of those dawn-tinted deluges of fire

Before their waves expire,
When heaven and earth are light, and only light
In the thunder-night!

VOICE WITHOUT:
Victory! Victory! Austria, Russia, England,
And that tame serpent, that poor shadow, France,
Cry peace, and that means death when monarchs speak.
Ho, there! bring torches, sharpen those red stakes,
These chains are light, fitter for slaves and poisoners
Than Greeks. Kill! plunder! burn! let none remain.

SEMICHORUS 1:
Alas! for Liberty!
If numbers, wealth, or unfulfilling years,
Or fate, can quell the free!
Alas! for Virtue, when
Torments, or contumely, or the sneers
Of erring judging men
Can break the heart where it abides.
Alas! if Love, whose smile makes this obscure world splendid,
Can change with its false times and tides,
Like hope and terror,
Alas for Love!
And Truth, who wanderest lone and unbefriended,
If thou canst veil thy lie-consuming mirror
Before the dazzled eyes of Error,
Alas for thee! Image of the Above.

SEMICHORUS 2:
Repulse, with plumes from conquest torn,
Led the ten thousand from the limits of the morn
Through many an hostile Anarchy!
At length they wept aloud, and cried, 'The Sea! the Sea!'
Through exile, persecution, and despair,
Rome was, and young Atlantis shall become
The wonder, or the terror, or the tomb
Of all whose step wakes Power lulled in her savage lair:
But Greece was as a hermit-child,
Whose fairest thoughts and limbs were built
To woman's growth, by dreams so mild,
She knew not pain or guilt;
And now, O Victory, blush! and Empire, tremble
When ye desert the free
If Greece must be
A wreck, yet shall its fragments reassemble,
And build themselves again impregnably
In a diviner clime,
To Amphionic music on some Cape sublime,
Which frowns above the idle foam of Time.

SEMICHORUS 1:
Let the tyrants rule the desert they have made;
Let the free possess the Paradise they claim;
Be the fortune of our fierce oppressors weighed
With our ruin, our resistance, and our name!

SEMICHORUS 2:
Our dead shall be the seed of their decay,
Our survivors be the shadow of their pride,
Our adversity a dream to pass away
Their dishonour a remembrance to abide!

VOICE WITHOUT:
Victory! Victory! The bought Briton sends
The keys of ocean to the Islamite.
Now shall the blazon of the cross be veiled,
And British skill directing Othman might,
Thunder-strike rebel victory. Oh, keep holy
This jubilee of unrevenged blood!
Kill! crush! despoil! Let not a Greek escape!

SEMICHORUS 1:
Darkness has dawned in the East
On the noon of time:
The death-birds descend to their feast
From the hungry clime.
Let Freedom and Peace flee far
To a sunnier strand,
And follow Love's folding-star
To the Evening land!

SEMICHORUS 2:
The young moon has fed
Her exhausted horn
With the sunset's fire:
The weak day is dead,
But the night is not born;
And, like loveliness panting with wild desire
While it trembles with fear and delight,
Hesperus flies from awakening night,
And pants in its beauty and speed with light
Fast-flashing, soft, and bright.
Thou beacon of love! thou lamp of the free!
Guide us far, far away,
To climes where now veiled by the ardour of day
Thou art hidden
From waves on which weary Noon
Faints in her summer swoon,
Between kingless continents sinless as Eden,
Around mountains and islands inviolably
Pranked on the sapphire sea.

SEMICHORUS 1:
Through the sunset of hope,
Like the shapes of a dream.
What Paradise islands of glory gleam!
Beneath Heaven's cope,
Their shadows more clear float by
The sound of their oceans, the light of their sky,
The music and fragrance their solitudes breathe
Burst, like morning on dream, or like Heaven on death,
Through the walls of our prison;
And Greece, which was dead, is arisen!

CHORUS:
The world's great age begins anew,
The golden years return,
The earth doth like a snake renew
Her winter weeds outworn:
Heaven smiles, and faiths and empires gleam,
Like wrecks of a dissolving dream.

A brighter Hellas rears its mountains
From waves serener far;
A new Peneus rolls his fountains
Against the morning star.
Where fairer Tempes bloom, there sleep
Young Cyclads on a sunnier deep.

A loftier Argo cleaves the main,
Fraught with a later prize;
Another Orpheus sings again,
And loves, and weeps, and dies.
A new Ulysses leaves once more
Calypso for his native shore.

Oh, write no more the tale of Troy,
If earth Death's scroll must be!
Nor mix with Laian rage the joy
Which dawns upon the free:
Although a subtler Sphinx renew
Riddles of death Thebes never knew.

Another Athens shall arise,
And to remoter time
Bequeath, like sunset to the skies,
The splendour of its prime;
And leave, if nought so bright may live,
All earth can take or Heaven can give.

Saturn and Love their long repose
Shall burst, more bright and good

Than all who fell, than One who rose,
Than many unsubdued:
Not gold, not blood, their altar dowers,
But votive tears and symbol flowers.

Oh, cease! must hate and death return?
Cease! must men kill and die?
Cease! drain not to its dregs the urn
Of bitter prophecy.
The world is weary of the past,
Oh, might it die or rest at last!

NOTES

(1) THE QUENCHLESS ASHES OF MILAN [L. 60].

Milan was the centre of the resistance of the Lombard league against the Austrian tyrant. Frederic Barbarossa burnt the city to the ground, but liberty lived in its ashes, and it rose like an exhalation from its ruin. See Sismondi's "Histoire des Republiques Italiennes", a book which has done much towards awakening the Italians to an imitation of their great ancestors.

(2) THE CHORUS [L. 197].

The popular notions of Christianity are represented in this chorus as true in their relation to the worship they superseded, and that which in all probability they will supersede, without considering their merits in a relation more universal. The first stanza contrasts the immortality of the living and thinking beings which inhabit the planets, and to use a common and inadequate phrase, "clothe themselves in matter", with the transience of the noblest manifestations of the external world.

The concluding verses indicate a progressive state of more or loss exalted existence, according to the degree of perfection which every distinct intelligence may have attained. Let it not be supposed that I mean to dogmatise upon a subject, concerning which all men are equally ignorant, or that I think the Gordian knot of the origin of evil can be disentangled by that or any similar assertions. The received hypothesis of a Being resembling men in the moral attributes of His nature, having called us out of non-existence, and after inflicting on us the misery of the commission of error, should superadd that of the punishment and the privations consequent upon it, still would remain inexplicable and incredible. That there is a true solution of the riddle, and that in our present state that solution is unattainable by us, are propositions which may be regarded as equally certain: meanwhile, as it is the province of the poet to attach himself to those ideas which exalt and ennoble humanity, let him be permitted to have conjectured the condition of that futurity towards which we are all impelled by an inextinguishable thirst for immortality. Until better arguments can be produced than sophisms which disgrace the cause, this desire itself must remain the strongest and the only presumption that eternity is the inheritance of every thinking being.

(3) NO HOARY PRIESTS AFTER THAT PATRIARCH [L. 245].

The Greek Patriarch, after having been compelled to fulminate an anathema against the insurgents, was put to death by the Turks.

Fortunately the Greeks have been taught that they cannot buy security by degradation, and the Turks, though equally cruel, are less cunning than the smooth-faced tyrants of Europe. As to the anathema, his Holiness might as well have thrown his mitre at Mount Athos for any effect that it produced. The chiefs of the Greeks are almost all men of comprehension and enlightened views on religion and politics.

(4) THE FREEDMAN OF A WESTERN POET-CHIEF [L. 563].

A Greek who had been Lord Byron's servant commands the insurgents in Attica. This Greek, Lord Byron informs me, though a poet and an enthusiastic patriot, gave him rather the idea of a timid and unenterprising person. It appears that circumstances make men what they are, and that we all contain the germ of a degree of degradation or of greatness whose connection with our character is determined by events.

(5) THE GREEKS EXPECT A SAVIOUR FROM THE WEST [L. 598].

It is reported that this Messiah had arrived at a seaport near Lacedaemon in an American brig. The association of names and ideas is irresistibly ludicrous, but the prevalence of such a rumour strongly marks the state of popular enthusiasm in Greece.

(6) THE SOUND AS OF THE ASSAULT OF AN IMPERIAL CITY [LL. 814-15].

For the vision of Mahmud of the taking of Constantinople in 1453, see Gibbon's "Decline and Fall of the Roman Empire", volume 12 page 223.

The manner of the invocation of the spirit of Mahomet the Second will be censured as over subtle. I could easily have made the Jew a regular conjuror, and the Phantom an ordinary ghost. I have preferred to represent the Jew as disclaiming all pretension, or even belief, in supernatural agency, and as tempting Mahmud to that state of mind in which ideas may be supposed to assume the force of sensations through the confusion of thought with the objects of thought, and the excess of passion animating the creations of imagination.

It is a sort of natural magic, susceptible of being exercised in a degree by anyone who should have made himself master of the secret associations of another's thoughts.

(7) THE CHORUS [L. 1060].

The final chorus is indistinct and obscure, as the event of the living drama whose arrival it foretells. Prophecies of wars, and rumours of wars, etc., may safely be made by poet or prophet in any age, but to anticipate however darkly a period of regeneration and happiness is a more hazardous exercise of the faculty which bards possess or feign. It will remind the reader 'magno NEC proximus intervallo' of Isaiah and Virgil, whose ardent spirits overleaping the actual reign of evil which we endure and bewail, already saw the possible and perhaps approaching state of society in which the 'lion shall lie down with the lamb,' and 'omnis feret omnia tellus.' Let these great names be my authority and my excuse.

(8) SATURN AND LOVE THEIR LONG REPOSE SHALL BURST [L. 1090].

Saturn and Love were among the deities of a real or imaginary state of innocence and happiness. ALL those WHO FELL, or the Gods of Greece, Asia, and Egypt; the ONE WHO ROSE, or Jesus Christ, at whose appearance the idols of the Pagan World wore amerced of their worship; and the MANY

UNSUBDUED, or the monstrous objects of the idolatry of China, India, the Antarctic islands, and the native tribes of America, certainly have reigned over the understandings of men in conjunction or in succession, during periods in which all we know of evil has been in a state of portentous, and, until the revival of learning and the arts, perpetually increasing, activity. The Grecian gods seem indeed to have been personally more innocent, although it cannot be said, that as far as temperance and chastity are concerned, they gave so edifying an example as their successor. The sublime human character of Jesus Christ was deformed by an imputed identification with a Power, who tempted, betrayed, and punished the innocent beings who were called into existence by His sole will; and for the period of a thousand years, the spirit of this most just, wise, and benevolent of men has been propitiated with myriads of hecatombs of those who approached the nearest to His innocence and wisdom, sacrificed under every aggravation of atrocity and variety of torture. The horrors of the Mexican, the Peruvian, and the Indian superstitions are well known.

NOTE ON HELLAS, BY MRS. SHELLEY.

The South of Europe was in a state of great political excitement at the beginning of the year 1821. The Spanish Revolution had been a signal to Italy; secrete societies were formed; and, when Naples rose to declare the Constitution, the call was responded to from Brundusium to the foot of the Alps. To crush these attempts to obtain liberty, early in 1821 the Austrians poured their armies into the Peninsula: at first their coming rather seemed to add energy and resolution to a people long enslaved. The Piedmontese asserted their freedom; Genoa threw off the yoke of the King of Sardinia; and, as if in playful imitation, the people of the little state of Massa and Carrara gave the conge to their sovereign, and set up a republic.

Tuscany alone was perfectly tranquil. It was said that the Austrian minister presented a list of sixty Carbonari to the Grand Duke, urging their imprisonment; and the Grand Duke replied, 'I do not know whether these sixty men are Carbonari, but I know, if I imprison them, I shall directly have sixty thousand start up.' But, though the Tuscans had no desire to disturb the paternal government beneath whose shelter they slumbered, they regarded the progress of the various Italian revolutions with intense interest, and hatred for the Austrian was warm in every bosom. But they had slender hopes; they knew that the Neapolitans would offer no fit resistance to the regular German troops, and that the overthrow of the constitution in Naples would act as a decisive blow against all struggles for liberty in Italy.

We have seen the rise and progress of reform. But the Holy Alliance was alive and active in those days, and few could dream of the peaceful triumph of liberty. It seemed then that the armed assertion of freedom in the South of Europe was the only hope of the liberals, as, if it prevailed, the nations of the north would imitate the example. Happily the reverse has proved the fact. The countries accustomed to the exercise of the privileges of freemen, to a limited extent, have extended, and are extending, these limits. Freedom and knowledge have now a chance of proceeding hand in hand; and, if it continue thus, we may hope for the durability of both. Then, as I have said, in 1821, Shelley, as well as every other lover of liberty, looked upon the struggles in Spain and Italy as decisive of the destinies of the world, probably for centuries to come. The interest he took in the progress of affairs was intense. When Genoa declared itself free, his hopes were at their highest. Day after day he read the bulletins of the Austrian army, and sought eagerly to gather tokens of its defeat. He heard of the revolt of Genoa with emotions of transport. His whole heart and soul were in the triumph of the cause. We were living at Pisa at that time; and several well-informed Italians, at the head of whom we may place the celebrated Vacca, were accustomed to seek for sympathy in their hopes from Shelley: they did not find such for the despair they too generally experienced, founded on contempt for their southern countrymen.

While the fate of the progress of the Austrian armies then invading Naples was yet in suspense, the news of another revolution filled him with exultation. We had formed the acquaintance at Pisa of several Constantinopolitan Greeks, of the family of Prince Caradja, formerly Hospodar of Wallachia; who, hearing that the bowstring, the accustomed finale of his viceroyalty, was on the road to him, escaped with his treasures, and took up his abode in Tuscany. Among these was the gentleman to whom the drama of "Hellas" is dedicated. Prince Mavrocordato was warmed by those aspirations for the independence of his country which filled the hearts of many of his countrymen. He often intimated the possibility of an insurrection in Greece; but we had no idea of its being so near at hand, when, on the 1st of April 1821, he called on Shelley, bringing the proclamation of his cousin, Prince Ypsilanti, and, radiant with exultation and delight, declared that henceforth Greece would be free.

Shelley had hymned the dawn of liberty in Spain and Naples, in two odes dictated by the warmest enthusiasm; he felt himself naturally impelled to decorate with poetry the uprise of the descendants of that people whose works he regarded with deep admiration, and to adopt the vaticinatory character in prophesying their success. "Hellas" was written in a moment of enthusiasm. It is curious to remark how well he overcomes the difficulty of forming a drama out of such scant materials. His prophecies, indeed, came true in their general, not their particular, purport. He did not foresee the death of Lord Londonderry, which was to be the epoch of a change in English politics, particularly as regarded foreign affairs; nor that the navy of his country would fight for instead of against the Greeks, and by the battle of Navarino secure their enfranchisement from the Turks. Almost against reason, as it appeared to him, he resolved to believe that Greece would prove triumphant; and in this spirit, auguring ultimate good, yet grieving over the vicissitudes to be endured in the interval, he composed his drama.

"Hellas" was among the last of his compositions, and is among the most beautiful. The choruses are singularly imaginative, and melodious in their versification. There are some stanzas that beautifully exemplify Shelley's peculiar style; as, for instance, the assertion of the intellectual empire which must be forever the inheritance of the country of Homer, Sophocles, and Plato:

'But Greece and her foundations are
Built below the tide of war,
Based on the crystalline sea
Of thought and its eternity.'

And again, that philosophical truth felicitously imaged forth -

'Revenge and Wrong bring forth their kind,
The foul cubs like their parents are,
Their den is in the guilty mind,
And Conscience feeds them with despair.'

The conclusion of the last chorus is among the most beautiful of his lyrics. The imagery is distinct and majestic; the prophecy, such as poets love to dwell upon, the Regeneration of Mankind and that regeneration reflecting back splendour on the foregone time, from which it inherits so much of intellectual wealth, and memory of past virtuous deeds, as must render the possession of happiness and peace of tenfold value.

www.ingramcontent.com/pod-product-compliance
Lightning Source LLC
Chambersburg PA
CBHW071314060426
42444CB00035B/2613